LADYBIRD HISTORIES

Tudors & Stuarts

History consultant: Philip Parker, historian and author
Map illustrator: Martin Sanders

A catalogue record for this book is available from the British Library

Published by Ladybird Books Ltd
80 Strand, London, WC2R 0RL
A Penguin Company

001

ISBN: 978-0-71819-621-9
Printed in China

LADYBIRD HISTORIES

Tudors & Stuarts

Written by Brian and Brenda Williams
Main illustrations by Carlo Molinari
Cartoon illustrations by Clive Goodyer

Contents

Tudor Family Tree   6

Stuart Family Tree   7

Introduction   8

Henry VIII   10

Henry and his Wives   12

Castles and Ships   14

Religion   16

Edward VI and Mary I   18

Elizabeth I   20

Mary, Queen of Scots   22

New Worlds   24

Plots and Wars   26

The Scottish King   28

The Gunpowder Plot   30

Shakespeare's England   32

Cavaliers and Roundheads   34

Civil War Battles   36

Return of the King 38

The Last Stuarts 40

Trade and Colonies 42

The Plague 44

The Great Fire of London 46

New Ideas 48

The Rich 50

The Poor 52

Childhood 54

Lasting Legacies 56

Timeline 58

Glossary 60

Places to Visit 63

Index 64

Tudor Family Tree

HENRY VII
1457–1509
RULED 1485–1509

ELIZABETH OF YORK
1466–1503

**ARTHUR TUDOR,
PRINCE OF WALES**
1486–1502

HENRY VIII
1491–1547
RULED 1509–1547

Henry VIII's wives
1. Catherine of Aragon m. 1509
2. Anne Boleyn m. 1533
3. Jane Seymour m. 1536
4. Anne of Cleves m. 1540
5. Katherine Howard m. 1540
6. Catherine Parr m. 1543

MARGARET TUDOR
1489–1541

**JAMES V
KING OF SCOTLAND**
1512–1542
RULED SCOTLAND 1513–1542

MARY TUDOR
1496–1533

**LADY FRANCES
BRANDON**
1517–1559

MARY I
1516–1558
RULED 1553–1558

ELIZABETH I
1533–1603
RULED 1558–1603
End of Tudor rule

EDWARD VI
1537–1553
RULED 1547–1553

MARY, QUEEN OF SCOTS
1542–1587
RULED SCOTLAND 1542–1567

LADY JANE GREY
1537–1554
RULED 1553
(FOR NINE DAYS)

Start of Stuart rule
**JAMES VI OF SCOTLAND AND
JAMES I OF ENGLAND**
1566–1625
RULED SCOTLAND 1567–1625
RULED ENGLAND 1603–1625

Stuart Family Tree

ANNE OF DENMARK
1574-1619

JAMES VI OF SCOTLAND
AND JAMES I OF ENGLAND
1566-1625

HENRY FREDERICK,
PRINCE OF WALES
1594-1612

ELIZABETH STUART
1596-1662

CHARLES LOUIS
1617-1680

PRINCE RUPERT
OF THE RHINE
1619-1682

SOPHIA OF HANOVER
1630-1714

CHARLES I
1600-1649
RULED 1625-1649

GEORGE I OF HANOVER
1660-1727
RULED 1714-1727

CHARLES II
1630-1685
RULED 1660-1685

MARY STUART
1631-1660

WILLIAM II
OF ORANGE
1626-1650

JAMES II
1633-1701
RULED 1685-1688

ELIZABETH
1635-1650

HENRY
1640-1660

HENRIETTA
ANNE
1644-1670

JOINT
SOVEREIGNS

PRINCE JAMES
FRANCIS EDWARD
1688-1766

WILLIAM III
1650-1702
RULED 1689-1702

MARY II
1662-1694
RULED 1689-1694

ANNE
1665-1714
RULED 1702-1714
End of Stuart rule

7

Introduction

Tudor and Stuart kings and queens ruled Britain for 229 years, from 1485 until 1714. Between 1460 and 1485, two royal families of Lancaster and York fought to rule England. This is known as the Wars of the Roses. At the Battle of Bosworth in 1485 Henry Tudor, of the House of Lancaster, won the crown of England from Richard III of York.

A family rose
The Lancastrians had a red rose badge. The York family rose was white. When the two families united so, too, was the rose.

The Battle of Bosworth in 1485 ended the Wars of the Roses.

Tudor rule

As king, the new ruler made his hold on the throne even stronger by marrying Elizabeth of York in 1486. Their son, Henry VIII, ruled next, and then Henry's children – Edward VI, Mary I and Elizabeth I. The Tudors ruled England until Elizabeth's death in 1603. Because she did not have any children, her closest relative, the Scottish King James VI, was next in line to the throne.

Stuart rule

King James VI became the first Stuart king of England, James I. He was followed by his son Charles I, who ruled from 1625 until he was executed during the Civil War in 1649. Charles's son Charles II, fled during these wars but returned as king in 1660. Charles II's brother, James II, was next in line, followed by joint sovereigns Mary II and her husband, William III. The last Stuart ruler was Queen Anne. When she died in 1714 the crown passed to George I of Hanover.

Henry VIII

Henry VII's eldest son, Arthur, died suddenly in 1502 when he was just fifteen years old. So when the king himself died in 1509, his younger son took the throne as Henry VIII.

Henry was born on 28 June 1491. He grew up to be a handsome and talented man. He wrote poetry and music, sang, danced, played tennis and was a fine athlete. But he was also vain, quick-tempered and a great show-off. In his later years King Henry VIII became fat, sick and a terrifying, cruel bully.

During his reign Henry VIII was determined to make England strong and show the world what a fine king he was. He was helped by able ministers, Cardinal Thomas Wolsey and chief minister Thomas Cromwell.

Henry VIII with Cardinal Wolsey (right) and Cromwell (left).

Court life

Henry wanted the best of everything. He spent money on palaces, clothes, jewels and feasts. In 1520 he went to meet King Francis I of France, near Calais. They stayed in a tent city so magnificent that it was called the Field of the Cloth of Gold. There, the kings tried to outdo one another with parties, jousts, wrestling matches and archery contests.

Henry and Francis met in a splendid tent city. When Henry heard of the French king's fine beard, he grew a beard, too!

Henry and his Wives

In 1509 Henry VIII married his brother's widow, Catherine of Aragon. But it would not be his only marriage. Desperate for a son and heir, the king would marry six times!

1. CATHERINE OF ARAGON

Henry and Catherine had six children, but only one lived – a girl called Mary. Henry wanted a son to rule after him. Henry decided to divorce Catherine but he needed the Pope, the head of the Roman Catholic Church, to agree. When the Pope refused, Henry decided to break away from the Pope and the Roman Catholic Church.

2. ANNE BOLEYN

Henry married his second wife, Anne Boleyn, in 1533. That year Anne had a daughter, Elizabeth. In 1536, believing stories of witchcraft and other lovers, Henry demanded Anne's death. She was sent to the Tower of London, where many important prisoners were executed. On 19 May 1536, Anne was beheaded with a sword.

3. JANE SEYMOUR

Henry's third wife was Anne Boleyn's lady-in-waiting, Jane Seymour. Henry seemed happy with Jane and she was perhaps his favourite. Jane gave birth to a son, Edward, in 1537. Henry was thrilled – he finally had his much longed-for heir. Sadly, just a few days later, the king would mourn the death of his wife.

To help you remember what happened to Henry's wives, say this rhyme:

Divorced, beheaded, died,
Divorced, beheaded, survived.

4. ANNE OF CLEVES

Henry then married Anne of Cleves in 1540. He had admired a portrait of Anne painted by the famous painter, Hans Holbein. But when they met she was not to his liking and Henry rudely said she looked like a horse! The marriage was annulled after just six months and Henry was free to choose another wife.

5. KATHERINE HOWARD

Henry's fifth wife was Katherine Howard. She was nineteen, he was forty nine. Lively and fun-loving, she made the king feel young again. But the queen was not aware of the ways of the court and she continued to have love affairs with other men after her marriage to the king. This eventually led to Katherine's execution in 1542.

6. CATHERINE PARR

Henry's last wife was Catherine Parr. The pair married in 1543 when, at fifty two, the king was in need of a gentle companion. Catherine fulfilled the role perfectly. She became an attentive stepmother to Henry's children as well as a compassionate carer for the now sick king, until Henry's death in 1547.

Castles and Ships

During Henry VIII's rule England fought wars with France and Scotland. He spent a lot of money building coastal castles to protect England from attack. Gunpowder had changed how wars were fought – now huge guns could knock down castle walls with cannonballs. To stop this, Henry's new castles had low walls with cannon to shoot at enemy ships.

Deal Castle in Kent looks like a Tudor rose, with six stone 'petals' surrounding a tower.

Great ships

During the Tudor period new ships were built for war, trade and exploring new lands. These ships were like floating castles. Scotland's King James IV had the *Great Michael* and Henry VIII had the *Great Harry*. These wooden warships had sails, guns and soldiers onboard, as well as sailors. The *Great Michael* could carry 1,400 people, most of them soldiers!

A sinking ship

Henry's most famous ship, the *Mary Rose*, sank off the coast of Portsmouth in 1545. The ship had too many soldiers onboard, making it top-heavy. As it leaned over, water poured in through the portholes. It is likely as many as 500 people onboard were drowned.

King Henry VIII watched from the shore as his ship sank to the bottom of the English Channel.

Raising the ship

In 1982 the wreck of the *Mary Rose* was raised from the seabed to be studied by archaeologists. What they found gave fascinating clues about Tudor life at sea. Razors, medical kits, shoes, musical instruments, bows and arrows, and even peapods were found in the wreckage!

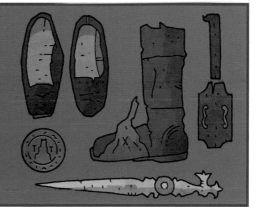

Religion

Religion was an important part of life in Tudor and Stuart times. Most people in western Europe were Christians. During the 1500s some people began to protest, wanting changes in the Roman Catholic Church. Many of these reformers left the Church and started the new Protestant Church. The split was called the Reformation.

Church of England

Most English and Scottish people belonged to the Roman Catholic Church, but felt the effects of this new Protestant movement. When Henry VIII wanted to divorce Catherine of Aragon (see page 12), he broke away from the Catholic Church and the Pope in Rome. Henry did not want to join the Protestants, but he did not agree with the Pope having authority in England. Instead, he made himself head of the Church in England in 1534.

Closing the monasteries

The Roman Catholic Church had lands and monasteries where monks lived and worked. Many monks would not accept the king as head of the Church of England. His officials told him monks were lazy and disobeyed church rules. He decided to close the monasteries and take away their land and treasures. All England's monasteries were closed by the time Henry died in 1547.

Henry's officials carry away monastery treasures.

17

Edward VI and Mary I

Following Henry's death in 1547, his son, Edward VI, became king. He was just nine years old, so his uncles Edward and Thomas Seymour ruled for him.

Edward was a sickly child and his illness was made worse by painful medical treatment. Sadly, Edward died in 1553 aged fifteen. The Duke of Northumberland wanted Lady Jane Grey to be queen next rather than Edward's eldest sister, Mary, who was a strict Roman Catholic. Jane was the granddaughter of Henry VIII's sister (see family tree, page 6), and married to the duke's son. She was queen for only nine days. Jane willingly gave up the throne to Edward's sister, Mary I, but was still executed in 1554.

Edward was nine years old when he became king in 1547. His eldest sister, Mary, was thirty years of age.

Mary I

Mary ruled from 1553 to 1558. A strict Roman Catholic, she wanted to turn England back to the Roman Catholic Church. During her reign many Protestants who would not give up their beliefs were burned at the stake. This earned her the nickname 'Bloody Mary'.

People were burned to death for their religious beliefs.

Six months after Mary came to the throne, she sent her younger sister, Elizabeth, to the Tower of London. Mary suspected Elizabeth of plotting against her. However, Mary had no proof and after two months Elizabeth was released from prison.

In 1554 Mary married Philip, who became king of Spain in 1556. They had no children, so when Mary died in 1558 Elizabeth became queen of England.

Elizabeth I

Queen Elizabeth I was the last of England's Tudor monarchs. She was born on 7 September 1533 to Henry VIII's second wife, Anne Boleyn. Elizabeth hardly knew her mother, who was executed in 1536. The princess grew up with her older sister, Mary. Red-haired and clever, like her father, Elizabeth learned French, Italian and Latin. She loved horse riding, hunting, playing music and dancing.

Queen Elizabeth I gave her name to the Elizabethan Age.

Good Queen Bess

As queen, Elizabeth faced many problems. There were plots to kill her and England was under the constant threat of invasion from France and Spain. Government spies, led by Sir Francis Walsingham, kept watch for plots that might harm Elizabeth.

Religion caused problems for the new queen, too. Mary I had been a strict Roman Catholic, but Elizabeth was a Protestant. England was once again a Protestant country. Roman Catholics had to attend Protestant church services, or pay fines if they refused. Some Roman Catholics worshipped in secret. They had private chapels in their homes and secret priest holes where priests hid to avoid capture.

Queen Elizabeth I was an intelligent, determined ruler, with able advisers. England grew stronger and richer during her reign. People loved and respected their monarch who became known as 'Good Queen Bess'.

Teeth, skin, wigs and baths!

Elizabeth had black, rotten teeth from eating too many sweetmeats. In old age she wore a red wig to hide her thin grey hair. As she aged, the queen also wore make-up to cover her smallpox scars and appear as young as possible in public. She would take four baths a year. This was considered a lot for the time!

Mary, Queen of Scots

Queen Elizabeth I and Mary, Queen of Scots, were cousins.
If Elizabeth died without having any children Mary, Queen
of Scots, would become Queen of England.

Mary was just a baby when her father, King James V, died
and she became Scotland's queen in 1542. In 1558 Mary
married Francis, the son of the French king. When Francis
became King of France in 1559, Mary found herself queen
of both Scotland and France.

After Francis's death in 1560 Mary returned to Scotland.
She married Henry Stewart, Lord Darnley in 1565 and
their son, James, was born in 1566. However, Darnley
became jealous of Mary's friendship with her secretary,
David Rizzio, and had him murdered. The following year
Darnley's house in Edinburgh was blown up and Darnley
was found dead in the garden.

Another husband

Mary then shocked people by marrying the Earl of Bothwell.
Many Scottish nobles thought he had planned Lord Darnley's
murder. In July 1567, these nobles forced Mary to give
up the throne. Her son, James, became King James VI of
Scotland, and Mary was locked up in Lochleven Castle.
She never saw her son again.

A cousin's help

In 1568 Mary sought protection from these Scottish nobles and fled to England, hoping for help from Elizabeth I. But Mary was a Roman Catholic and some English Roman Catholics felt she should be England's queen instead of Elizabeth. Fearing Mary might try to take her throne, the queen kept Mary prisoner for almost nineteen years.

Mary became involved in a Catholic plot against Elizabeth. An English Roman Catholic, Sir Anthony Babington, wanted Elizabeth to be killed and Mary made queen of England. But Walsingham's spies got hold of letters from Mary to the plotters and learned about the scheme. Her fate was sealed. Elizabeth signed Mary's death warrant and she was executed in 1587.

Mary was kept prisoner in Fotheringhay Castle, Northamptonshire.

New Worlds

The Elizabethan age was a time of overseas discovery. English captains sailed to the Americas and ships even sailed to the Arctic. Explorers had hoped to find a new sea route to China and India but were beaten by the ice. England and Spain were still enemies and often attacked one another's ships. English ships took so much gold and silver from the Spanish that they called the English 'pirates'.

A sailor's job was tough and life at sea was dangerous. Men often died in fights with the Spanish, fell from masts, were washed overboard, died of disease or drowned if their ship sank. Boys as young as ten were cabin boys.

Life at sea

Food onboard crawled with maggots. Drinking water was slimy and smelly, so sailors drank beer instead. In fact most Tudors drank beer, which was less likely to make them sick than dirty water.

Francis Drake

During Elizabeth's rule Francis Drake became the first English sea captain to sail around the world, although only one of his five ships completed the round trip.

As well as a great explorer, Drake was a fierce fighter. He attacked Spanish ports in America and sailed home with his ship crammed with gold taken from the Spanish. Queen Elizabeth was delighted and knighted him on board his ship, the *Golden Hinde*. To the English he was Sir Francis Drake, the hero, but the Spanish called him 'el draque' – the dragon!

Francis Drake sailed the Pacific Ocean in his ship, the *Golden Hinde*.

Plots and Wars

In 1587 England was in danger of attack from Spain, Europe's strongest country. Spain's King Philip II was a Roman Catholic and wanted England to be a Roman Catholic country once more, and under Spain's control. First he had to get rid of Queen Elizabeth…

Philip plotted to put Mary, Queen of Scots, on the English throne, but the scheme failed and Mary was executed in 1587. The king needed a new plan. In May 1588 a fleet of 130 ships, carrying 130,000 sailors and soldiers, known as the Armada, set sail to attack the English.

The Spanish Armada

Elizabeth's fleet of about 200 ships sailed to do battle
with the Spanish in the English Channel. Both sides fought
bravely. The main battles took place in the sea near Calais,
France, in early August. The English sent fireships into the
Armada to scatter the enemy vessels. After one last battle,
a storm blew the Spanish Armada north, forcing them to
sail round Scotland. Many were damaged as they navigated
the rocky coastline of Ireland. Less than half managed to get
back to Spain and England was saved from invasion.

Armada facts
* The Armada had 2,500 big guns,
  or cannon, and 7,000 handguns.
* Only about sixty Spanish ships
  returned home to Spain.
* The Spanish did not sink any
  English ships.

The Scottish King

On 24 March 1603 Queen Elizabeth I died. Her reign is remembered as one of the most glorious in English history. Upon her death, a message was sent to Scotland, telling King James VI that he was now James I of England, too. James hurried south. Many English people welcomed him as king, even though they struggled to understand his Scottish accent. He was often clumsy and even stumbled during his coronation!

A strong-minded king

James had strong views. He believed kings were chosen by God and could do what they liked. He expected Parliament to obey him without question. When England's Parliament refused to give him money, James began selling land and titles to his friends to raise the funds he needed. He quickly became unpopular in England.

The king was well-educated and very clever. In 1611 he authorized a new translation of the Bible from Latin into English, known today as the King James Bible.

Demonology

The Tudors and Stuarts believed in devils and witches, and King James I even wrote a book on demonology in 1597. If a woman was thought to be a witch she could be dunked or ducked in a pond. If she did not drown, it was believed she must have witch's powers!

James VI rides south from Scotland to become James I of England.

29

The Gunpowder Plot

James had been king of England for just two years when there was an attack on his life – the Gunpowder Plot of 1605. Roman Catholics in England had hoped that King James I would weaken anti-Catholic laws. When he did not, thirteen men plotted to blow up Parliament in November 1605.

The plotters smuggled gunpowder in boats across the River Thames to Westminster. They then stacked the barrels in a cellar below Parliament. The group's gunpowder expert was a soldier called Guy Fawkes. He hid in the cellar on 4 November, waiting to light the fuse and set off the powder the next day.

Betrayed!

The plot was betrayed when a letter was sent to Lord Monteagle, warning him not to attend Parliament on 5 November. Lord Monteagle told Robert Cecil, the king's chief minister. Cecil had the cellar searched and Guy Fawkes was arrested. When he was tortured he confessed to the plot and revealed the names of the other plotters. They had already fled London. Some were caught and others were killed by soldiers at a house in Staffordshire.

A sticky end

Those who were caught, including Guy Fawkes, were hanged, drawn and quartered. This consisted of being hanged, taken down still alive, cut into four pieces and the head stuck on a pole. This terrible punishment was a warning to others.

Guy Fawkes was arrested in the cellars underneath Parliament
before he could light the fuse to the gunpowder.

Bonfire Night

After the plot was foiled people
lit bonfires to celebrate the
king's escape. On 5 November
every year, people still light
bonfires to remember the
Gunpowder Plot.

Shakespeare's England

The playwright William Shakespeare was writing during the reigns of Queen Elizabeth I and King James I. Shakespeare was born in Stratford-upon-Avon in 1564. His mother, Mary Arden, was a farmer's daughter. His father, John Shakespeare, made gloves and was a leading citizen of the town.

Shakespeare married Anne Hathaway in 1582 and had three children. Very little is known about his early life. We know he was writing plays in London in the 1590s. In between he may have been a travelling actor, a tutor to a rich family, a soldier or a sailor. Nobody knows!

London's theatres

Theatre was very popular with both the rich and the poor. Queen Elizabeth I and King James I enjoyed watching plays, too. When James came to London, the actors from Shakespeare's Globe Theatre became known as the King's Men. They even walked in the king's coronation procession.

By 1611 Shakespeare was rich and famous and he had retired home to Stratford. He died on 23 April 1616, aged fifty two.

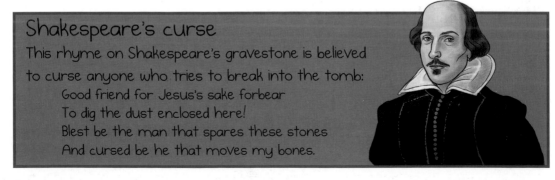

Shakespeare's curse
This rhyme on Shakespeare's gravestone is believed to curse anyone who tries to break into the tomb:
Good friend for Jesus's sake forbear
To dig the dust enclosed here!
Blest be the man that spares these stones
And cursed be he that moves my bones.

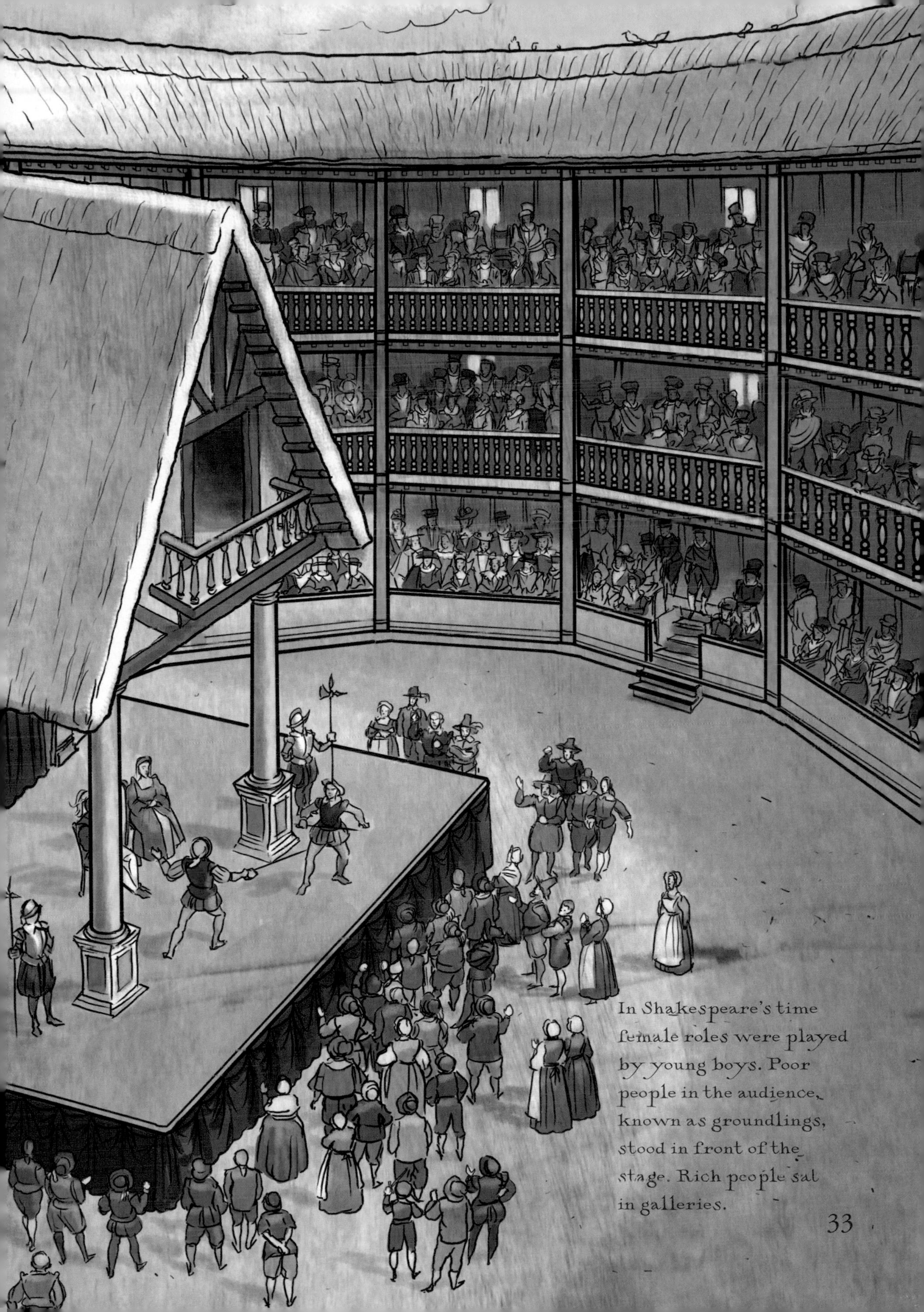

In Shakespeare's time
female roles were played
by young boys. Poor
people in the audience,
known as groundlings,
stood in front of the
stage. Rich people sat
in galleries.

33

Cavaliers and Roundheads

When James I died in 1625 his son Charles I became king. The new king quarrelled with Parliament, mainly over money and religion. In 1629 Charles decided to rule without Parliament, because it would not agree to the taxes he wanted to impose. These new taxes made people angry and the king became very unpopular. Many English and Scottish people also feared that the king would make both countries Roman Catholic once more. Charles's wife, Henrietta Maria of France, was a Roman Catholic.

When Charles I needed money in 1640 he was forced to recall Parliament. Members of Parliament (MPs) still did not do what the king wanted, even when he tried to arrest five of them. In 1642 Charles left London to raise an army against Parliament. Civil War had begun.

Cavaliers
Cavaliers had long hair and dressed in fine clothes.

Roundheads
Roundheads were so called because of their closely cropped hair. They wore plain clothes.

Civil War

The king's followers were 'Cavaliers' or Royalists. Parliament's followers were 'Roundheads' who, led by Oliver Cromwell, soon got the upper hand. The king sought help from the Scots, but they handed him over to Parliament in exchange for £400,000 – a lot of money for the time! The king managed to escape, but was soon recaptured and imprisoned again. Even as a prisoner he tried to restart the war. In the end Charles was put on trial for treason by Parliament. He was found guilty and beheaded on 30 January 1649.

King Charles I did not want to shiver in the bitter January cold and appear frightened, so he wore an extra shirt to his execution.

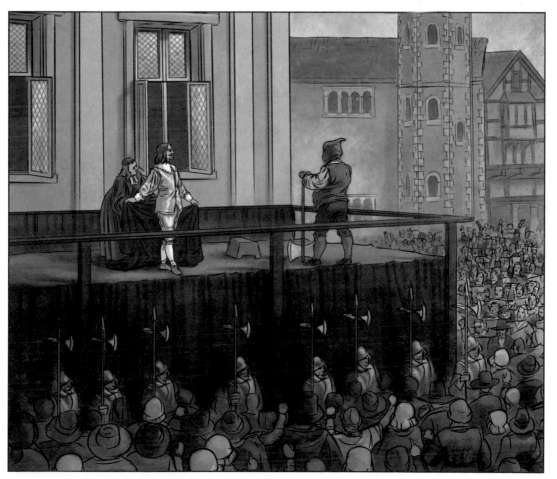

Civil War Battles

The Civil War years were deadly. There were a few big battles, and lots of smaller ones. At first, the king's army had more trained soldiers. Parliament then formed the New Model Army, led by Oliver Cromwell. Cromwell's 'Ironsides', as they were called, were soon even better than the Cavaliers.

Roundheads and Cavaliers had similar weapons. In battle, foot soldiers carried long spears or pikes. Some had handguns, called muskets, which were like rifles. Armies marched into battle with drums beating and flags flying. Cavalry fired pistols, and used swords and long-handled poleaxes as they charged into the well-drilled lines of foot soldiers. Artillery soldiers fired cannon, making clouds of smoke.

There were Civil War battles in England, Scotland, Wales and Ireland. Royalists hoped for Ireland's support against Parliament, even after the death of Charles I, but Cromwell had brutally crushed Irish resistance by 1652.

Big Battles of the Civil War

1642 Edgehill – Royalist win

1644 Marston Moor – Parliament win

1645 Naseby – Parliament win

1651 Worcester – Parliament win.
Cromwell defeats Charles II and the Scots

MAP KEY
✗ Royalist win
✗ Parliament win

At Edgehill in 1642, Sir Edmund Verney (a Cavalier) fought against his son Ralph (a Roundhead). Sir Edmund was killed in the battle even though it was a Royalist win.

Charles II's escape

The Scots had their own army. During the war they changed sides: first backing Charles I, then siding with Parliament. After the king's execution the Scots tried to help Charles's son, Charles II. But Cromwell beat the Scots. After losing the Battle of Worcester in England in 1651, the young Charles II hid in a tree before escaping in disguise to France.

Return of the King

After King Charles I was executed in 1649 Britain became a commonwealth. Oliver Cromwell ruled as Lord Protector from 1653 until his death in 1658.

Life under the Commonwealth was shaped by the Puritans. Laws were passed banning games, dancing, theatres and, at one stage, even Christmas dinner!

Cromwell's son, Richard, became Lord Protector in 1658, but he was weak and unpopular. Many people hated the Puritan laws and wanted life to return to how it used to be. In 1660 Parliament invited Charles I's son Charles II, to return as king. Crowds cheered his return. This is called the Restoration.

The Merry Monarch

Charles II liked sport, the theatre and dancing. He took an interest in science, too. The Royal Society (for scientists) was founded in 1660, and Charles also set up the Royal Observatory in Greenwich in 1675. With the Restoration, Parliament had been given more power, but the king was popular and in England he became known as the Merry Monarch!

The royal lab
King Charles II had his own laboratory and even enjoyed carrying out science experiments himself!

Charles II brought music and dancing back to court.

The life of a mistress

King Charles II had many mistresses. Nell Gwyn is one of the most famous. She originally sold oranges at the Theatre Royal in Drury Lane, before becoming an actress at the age of fifteen. One day she caught the eye of the king and was soon enjoying life as his mistress.

The Last Stuarts

CHARLES II

Charles II was a fun-loving monarch. He introduced champagne to England and opened up theatres that had been closed during Cromwell's Puritan rule.

The king was charming and good-looking, too. In 1662 he married Catherine of Braganza, the daughter of the king of

Portugal. He had affairs, lots of mistresses and possibly as many as fourteen illegitimate children. But the queen did not have any children so, when Charles died in 1685, he had no legitimate heir to the throne.

JAMES II

It was Charles's brother, James, who succeeded him. If Charles had been the 'Merry Monarch', James II was 'Dismal Jimmy'. He was a Roman Catholic, and Parliament did not want him as king.

In 1688 James's second wife, Mary of Modena, gave birth to a son. This caused alarm among Protestants. A story spread that the baby was not the queen's, but had been smuggled into the palace by plotters! Such fears added to James's unpopularity.

Mary II and William III of Orange

Parliament offered the crown to James II's eldest daughter Mary, who was a Protestant, and her Dutch husband, William III of Orange. When William arrived with his army in 1688, James fled to France. Called the Glorious Revolution, William and Mary officially ruled from 1689.

After Mary II's death in 1694 William III ruled alone until 1702. Not everyone welcomed William III as sole monarch. James's supporters wanted James II to return, or another Stuart king to rule. When William fell from his horse to his death as it stumbled over a molehill, James's supporters drank toasts to the mole!

Queen Anne

Following William's death, James II's youngest daughter, Anne, became queen. During her reign the Acts of Union in 1707 united England and Scotland under one Parliament.

The queen and her husband, Prince George of Denmark, had a happy marriage, but sadly Anne lost many children during her life. She died without an heir in 1714 so the crown passed to George I, ruler of the German state of Hanover. Stuart rule in Great Britain was over.

Trade and Colonies

The adventurer Sir Walter Raleigh set up England's first colonies in the New World of America in 1585 and 1587. These colonies did not last but, in 1607, an English settlement in Jamestown, Virginia, was established and survived. Then, in 1620, 102 Puritan men, women and children set sail from Plymouth, England, in a ship called the *Mayflower*. They started another colony at Plymouth, Massachusetts.

More people settled along the east coast of America. They prospered through fishing, fur trapping and tobacco-growing until there were thirteen British colonies. In 1776 these colonies broke away from British rule to become the United States of America.

East coast
of USA

Atlantic Ocean

KEY
1 – Massachusetts
2 – New Hampshire
3 – New York
4 – Rhode Island
5 – Connecticut
6 – New Jersey
7 – Pennsylvania
8 – Delaware
9 – Maryland
10 – Virginia
11 – North Carolina
12 – South Carolina
13 – Georgia

IN 1820 THE NORTHERN AREA OF MASSACHUSETTS BECAME THE STATE OF MAINE. BEFORE THAT IT WAS PART OF THE MASSACHUSETTS COLONY.

British trade

Throughout the Tudor and Stuart periods overseas trade was booming. Spain and Portugal had control of trade across the Southern Atlantic Ocean and around the coast of Africa, so English seamen and explorers were keen to search north for new routes to Asia. British ships brought back foods and drinks, such as 'China drink' or 'Tay' (tea). In the early 1600s coffee arrived in England and quickly became more popular than beer!

One company, the East India Company, became so powerful it controlled British trade with much of Asia. It made some British people very rich, and by the 1700s the company even ruled parts of India!

Possibly the most valuable trade route at this time was the 'trade triangle'. British ships traded iron and guns for African slaves, which they brought to the New World. They then returned to England with sugar, cotton and tobacco.

The Plague

In the unusually hot summer of 1665 a deadly disease, called the plague, swept across London. With no medicines to cure the disease, a third of London's population died.

The bubonic plague was spread by fleas that lived on rats in the city. The filthy, narrow streets of London were perfect for rats to breed and spread disease. The plague caused painful swellings in the groin and armpits, blotches on the skin and fever. Most people died quickly, but it was a painful death. A house with a red cross painted on the door meant a plague victim was inside. The home was shut up to stop infection spreading and anyone inside was left to die.

Doctors wore long coats, gloves and pointed masks, like birds' beaks, filled with scented herbs. They hoped the herbs would protect them.

Burying the dead

People lit bonfires in an attempt to 'clean the air', and many people fled to the countryside. By August about 1,000 plague victims were dying every day. Men drove carts through the streets, shouting 'Bring out your dead'. Then the bodies were tipped into large pits. Only when winter came did the plague stop. About 100,000 people had died.

Samuel Pepys worked in London for the Navy.
He kept a diary in which he wrote about the plague:

'Thus this month ends, with great sadness upon the public through the greateness of the plague, everywhere through the Kingdom almost. Every day sadder and sadder news of its increase.'

The Great Fire of London

In 1666, just a year after the plague, Britain's biggest city faced a new disaster. Fire! On 2 September 1666, a fire broke out in a baker's shop in Pudding Lane. Fanned by a breeze, the flames soon spread through the narrow streets of wooden houses.

People fought the blaze with pumps and buckets of water from the River Thames. Many fled with all they could carry or load into carts. Others crowded into boats on the river. Eventually, King Charles II ordered houses to be blown up to make gaps and so stopped the fire spreading.

About 100,000 people lost their homes, but only nine people died. Hospitals and churches, including St Paul's Cathedral, were destroyed in the fire.

London's burning

London burned for four days and nights. After the fire the king asked an architect, Sir Christopher Wren, to help rebuild the city. Wren made sure the new streets were wider and that buildings were made of brick or stone. His new St Paul's Cathedral took thirty six years to build. Sir Christopher Wren was buried there when he died at the age of ninety in 1723.

Saving the cheese

Samuel Pepys also wrote about the fire in his diary. Before leaving his house to escape the flames, Pepys buried wine and some Parmesan cheese in his garden to save it from the fire!

New Ideas

In an age of new ideas and discoveries, scientists and explorers learned more about the world. At the beginning of the Tudor period English artists, writers and scientists began to learn about, and be influenced by, Renaissance styles and ideas from Europe.

During James I's reign scientists began to carry out more scientific experiments. By the end of the period more was known about the human body, nature and the planets than ever before. The Italian scientist Galileo Galilei was the first to look at the moon through a telescope in 1609. In Britain, William Harvey showed how the heart pumps blood around the body. Isaac Newton, Robert Boyle, Robert Hooke and Edmund Halley discovered lots about maths, physics, chemistry and astronomy. John Locke and Thomas Hobbes had new ideas about government, and the microscope, barometer and pendulum clock were all invented.

Isaac Newton

In 1687 Isaac Newton published his book Principia. In it he explained his ideas about motion, gravity and time. A famous story says he once saw an apple fall from a tree and wondered why it fell. The answer was gravity.

A slow pace of life

Despite these new discoveries, the pace of life was still slow.
Nothing went faster than a galloping horse or a ship under
sail, and it took nearly four days to travel from London to
York in the north of England.

Roads in Britain were very bad and repairs were not often
carried out. As a result the roads were full of holes and
stagecoaches often became stuck or overturned.

The quickest and safest way to travel was by water. Goods
travelled by barge along rivers and the Thames was like a busy
road. Still, while merchants, sailors and settlers crossed oceans,
most people seldom left their home town or village.

The streets were dark and dangerous at night. Wealthy people often
paid a link-boy to walk in front of them.

The Rich

The Tudor and Stuart periods saw trade across the country and overseas grow, and a few people became very rich during the reign of the Tudor ruler, Queen Elizabeth I. They were keen to show off their wealth and built large homes, some in the shape of an 'E' for Elizabeth. Later, wealthy Stuarts carried on building big houses with large landscaped gardens.

By the 1600s houses were being built from brick or stone, and had lots of rooms. Rich people had carpets on the floors, wooden panels on walls, elegant paintings and big staircases. They had carved wooden chests in which to store things, wooden tables, and chairs with padded seats and leather backs.

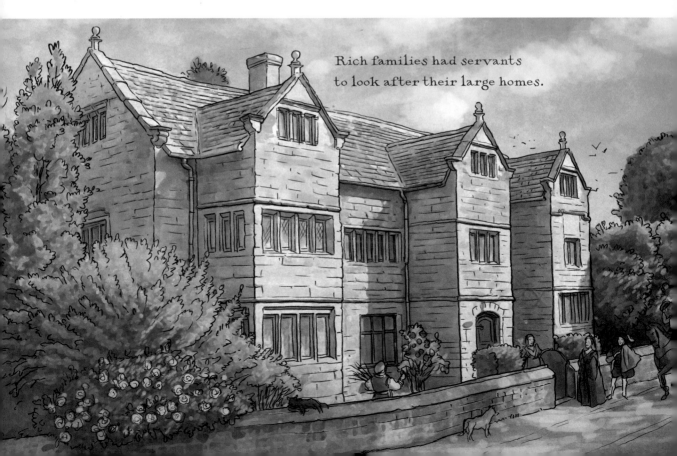

Rich families had servants to look after their large homes.

Food

A rich family might offer visitors a dinner of carp, ox-tongue, roast chicken, goose pie, pigeons, oysters and syllabub. Dinner guests brought their own spoons, and perhaps a fork – the latest fashion from Italy.

Clothes

Rich women could afford beautiful dresses, such as the Tudor farthingale, a bell-shaped skirt over a hooped frame. Wealthy Tudor men liked gold earrings and ruffs. Stuarts wore silk jackets with lace cuffs and coloured ribbons.

Gentlemen during Henry VIII's reign wore padded jackets, called doublets, and woollen tights. Ladies wore velvet gowns and jewelled headdresses.

1509–1547

1558–1603

During the Stuart period clothes lost their stiffness and ribbons became popular decorations.

1603–1714

Elizabethan women wore stiff collars called ruffs, which were supported by wire frames. Men dressed in short padded trousers called breeches.

The Poor

Life for poor families was very hard. Many people got up at dawn and went to bed soon after dark, because candles were expensive to use at night. Breakfast was a snack of bread and beer or milk. Lunch was at about eleven or twelve o'clock. It might be pottage or bread, bacon and peas or beans. Potato pie was a treat! Supper was at six o'clock or when the day's work was done.

Dirty times

Soap was a luxury during Tudor and Stuart times and there was no running water. Maybe once a year people would fill a copper tub full of water heated by the fire in order to take a bath. More than one person would use the same bathwater! The toilet was usually outside, it was called a privy. During the night people would use a chamber pot, stored under the bed.

In the morning the waste from the chamber pot was thrown out from windows high above the street!

Hard work

Many poor people worked as servants, farm hands, sailors and labourers. Those without work or money often turned to begging in the street. The punishment for being a beggar or vagabond was to be burned through the gristle of the right ear with a hot iron. If caught again, then the other ear got the same treatment. Others turned to crime, risking even harsher punishments. A thief might have an ear cut off and his nose slit. Highwaymen were hanged and their bodies displayed in cages as a warning to others. To help the poor, The Poor Act was passed by Parliament in 1552. As a result workhouses were set up, where people could work in exchange for food and shelter.

Clothes

Most people wore plain clothes. They could not afford the latest fashions but made do with whatever material they could find. Clothes would be patched and mended by the women of the house – nothing was ever thrown away!

Sounds of the street

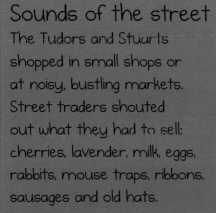

The Tudors and Stuarts shopped in small shops or at noisy, bustling markets. Street traders shouted out what they had to sell: cherries, lavender, milk, eggs, rabbits, mouse traps, ribbons, sausages and old hats.

Childhood

There were very few formal schools in Tudor and Stuart times. Rich children had lessons at home, learning subjects such as Latin, history and geography. They would also study literature and the Bible, while most poor people never even learned to read or write.

Only a few poor children were lucky enough to go to school. Many boys learned their father's trade from as young as ten years old. Others left home to become an apprentice or perhaps to go to sea. Girls learned to cook and run a home. Most were married by the age of fourteen.

Rich children were schooled at home by tutors.

Poor children worked hard at home. Girls cooked, sewed and cleaned. Boys, like this blacksmith's son, helped with the family trade.

Toys and leisure time

Rich families could afford life-like dolls, toy horses, drums and model ships. Poor children made their own games and played with homemade toys. Rag dolls, skittles, stilts, hoops and marbles were favourites.

Most children loved the travelling fair with its acrobats, jugglers, fire-eaters and, perhaps, a dancing bear. On holy days everyone joined in shows, races and games. Travelling actors put on plays in the town square.

Lasting Legacies

Life changed for people during the Tudor and Stuart period. When the Tudor age began in the late 1400s knights still wore armour to war. As the Stuart age ended in the early 1700s guns had made armour old-fashioned. The world seemed smaller, with ships sailing the oceans and telescopes able to look at the moon and stars far above in the sky.

After the long years of Civil War in the 1600s, power shifted from the king to Parliament. England and Scotland had the same king from 1603, but separate parliaments until they were united in 1707 in the Acts of Union.

A time of splendour

Religion was important in public and at home. Great churches were built, such as St Paul's Cathedral. The growing wealth of the period is still visible in beautiful buildings, such as Hampton Court Palace and Holyrood House, and country houses like Blenheim and Chatsworth. You can still visit these magnificent places today.

The Tudors and Stuarts gave us famous kings and queens, explorers and soldiers, scientists and artists. Of the great writers, none was greater than Shakespeare. Explorers sailed the oceans, and settlers founded some of the colonies that grew into the British Empire.

Important events to remember

1485

End of the Wars of the Roses. Henry VII comes to the throne. Start of Tudor rule.

1534

Act of Supremacy that sees Henry VIII becoming the head of the Church of England.

1588

The Spanish Armada takes place with England victorious against the Spanish.

1603

King James VI of Scotland becomes the first Stuart king – James I.

1605

An attempt is made to blow up Parliament in the infamous Gunpowder Plot.

1642–51

The long Civil War years fought between the Cavaliers and the Roundheads.

1665

The plague comes to London, killing about 100,000 people.

1666

The Great Fire of London destroys England's biggest city.

1714

Queen Anne dies. Stuart rule in England is over as George I of Hanover becomes King of England.

Timeline

1485	Henry Tudor wins the Battle of Bosworth, declaring himself King of England. By defeating Richard III, Henry ends the Wars of the Roses
1488	James III of Scotland is killed fighting. His son becomes James IV
1492	Christopher Columbus sails from Spain to the West Indies
1497	English sailors led by the Italian, John Cabot, sail to North America
1498	Vasco da Gama of Portugal is the first European sailor to reach India
1500	The Renaissance is at its height in Europe
1509	Henry VIII becomes King of England
1517	Martin Luther starts the Protestant movement against the Roman Catholic Church
1519–22	The first round-the-world voyage, by the Portuguese explorer, Ferdinand Magellan, and his crew
1534	Henry VIII makes himself head of the Church of England
1543	Polish scientist Nicolaus Copernicus says the Earth moves around the sun
1547	Henry VIII dies. Edward VI becomes King of England
1553	Lady Jane Grey is queen for nine days after Edward VI dies, but is beheaded when Mary I becomes queen
1553–58	Protestants in England are persecuted while Mary I is queen
1558	Elizabeth I becomes Queen of England
1580	Francis Drake's ship, the *Golden Hinde* reaches home after a three-year voyage around the world
1587	Mary, Queen of Scots, is beheaded in England
1588	The English defeat the Spanish Armada

1592	Shakespeare is writing his plays in London
1603	Queen Elizabeth I dies. James VI of Scotland becomes James I of England, its first Stuart king
1605	The Gunpowder Plot
1607	The English start a colony in Virginia, America
1611	The King James Bible is published
1620	Puritan men, women and children sail to America in the *Mayflower*
1625	Charles I becomes king
1642	Civil War begins in England between King Charles I (and the Cavaliers) and Parliament (and the Roundheads)
1649	Charles I is beheaded
1651	Charles II flees to France
1653	Oliver Cromwell becomes Lord Protector. England is ruled as a commonwealth
1660	The Restoration: King Charles II returns to England
1665	The Great Plague
1666	The Great Fire of London
1685	King Charles II dies. His brother becomes King James II
1688	King James II flees. His daughter Mary II and her husband, William III reign
1694	Mary II dies. William rules alone as king until his death in 1702
1702	Mary's sister Anne becomes queen
1707	The Acts of Union unite the kingdoms of England and Scotland to form Great Britain
1714	Queen Anne, the last Stuart ruler, dies. George I becomes England's king, first of the house of Hanover

Glossary

annul	to cancel a marriage
apprentice	a young person learning a trade
archaeologist	someone who studies the past from objects and other evidence
beggar	a poor person asking for help, food or money
behead	to cut off someone's head
blacksmith	a person who makes and repairs things in iron by hand
cannon	a big gun used to fire solid cannonballs
cavalry	soldiers on horseback
chamber pot	a pot used as a toilet during the night
chapel	a small church, sometimes just a room
colony	a settlement in another country
Commonwealth	the republic that existed in Britain from 1649 to 1660
coronation	crowning a king or queen at the start of their reign
demonology	the study of demons and witches
divorce	to end a marriage by law
execute	put to death by law as punishment
farthingale	a structure worn under a woman's dress to give it shape
fireship	a ship set on fire and sent to scatter enemy vessels
gunpowder	an explosive made from chemicals

heir	someone who is legally entitled to the rank of another on that person's death
highwayman	someone who robs travellers on the road
illegitimate	born to unmarried parents
inherit	to receive money, property or a title on the death of another person
joust	a sporting contest between two knights, or men on horseback, as they fight with lances
labourer	someone who works with their hands or simple tools
Latin	the language of the ancient Romans
legitimate	born of legally married parents
link-boy	a boy who carried a torch at night for money
Lord Protector	someone in charge of a kingdom during the absence of the king or queen
merchant	a person who makes money by buying and selling goods
mistress	a woman acting as a wife, though not married
monarch	a ruler, such as a king or queen
monastery	somewhere monks or nuns live, work and pray
New Model Army	the army created in 1645 by Oliver Cromwell
Parliament	an assembly of the nobility, clergy and commons called together by the British sovereign. The place where laws are made
pendulum clock	a clock regulated by a weighted swinging lever

Glossary

Pope	head of the Roman Catholic church
porthole	a small hole on the outside of a ship
pottage	a kind of soup or stew
priest hole	a hiding place for a Roman Catholic priest during times of religious difficulty
prosper	to gain wealth
Puritan	Protestant person living by strict rules
recall Parliament	the act of officially bringing Parliament back. Charles I dismissed and then recalled Parliament during his reign
reformer	someone who makes changes
reign	the period of time (in years) a king or queen rules
Renaissance	the revival of European art and literature in the 1500s and 1600s
resistance	the refusal to accept something
Restoration	the re-establishment of King Charles II as king of England in 1660
settler	a person living in a new land
slave	a person who works for no wages and is owned by another
sovereign	a ruler, such as a king or queen
stagecoach	a large covered horse-drawn carriage used to carry messages or people long distances
sweetmeat	an item of sweet food
succession	to follow or replace someone

syllabub	a whipped-cream dessert, typically flavoured with white wine or sherry
title	a name or description of rank
treason	the crime of betraying your country
tutor	a teacher for a family, rather than in a school
vagabond	a person who wanders from place to place without a home or a job

Places to Visit

Blenheim Palace, Oxfordshire
Chatsworth House, Derbyshire
Hampton Court Palace, London
Holyrood House, Edinburgh, Scotland
Kenilworth Castle, Warwickshire
Leeds Castle, Kent
National Maritime Museum and the Royal Observatory, London
Shakespeare's Globe, London
Stratford-upon-Avon, Staffordshire
Tower of London, London
Windsor Castle, Berkshire

For more information about the Tudors and Stuarts and other resources, visit **www.ladybird.com**

Index

America 24, 25, 42–3
Anne, Queen 9, 41, 57
Aragon, Catherine of 12, 16

Boleyn, Anne 12, 20

castles 14, 22, 23
Cavaliers 34–7, 57
Charles I, King 9, 34–7, 38
Charles II, King 9, 36–7, 38–9, 40, 46, 47
childhood 54–5
Church of England 16, 57
Civil War 9, 34–7, 56, 57
Cleves, Anne of 13
clothes 11, 34, 51, 53
colonies 42–43
Commonwealth 38
Cromwell, Oliver 35, 36, 37, 38, 40

Drake, Francis 25

Edward VI, King 9, 12, 18
Elizabeth I, Queen 9, 12, 19, 20–8, 50
exploration 24–5, 42, 43, 48, 56

food 24, 43, 51, 52, 53

Glorious Revolution 41
Great Fire of London 46–7, 57
Gunpowder Plot 30–1, 57

Henry VII, King 8, 10, 48, 57
Henry VIII, King 9, 10–17, 18, 57
Howard, Katherine 13

Ironsides 36

James I, King 9, 22, 28–31, 32, 34, 48, 57
James II, King 9, 40–1
James IV, King 14
James V, King 22
James VI, King *see* James I, King
Jane Grey, Lady 18

King James Bible 28

Mayflower 42
Mary I, Queen 9, 12, 18–9, 21
Mary II, Queen and William III 9, 41
Mary Rose 15
Mary, Queen of Scots 22–3, 26

New Model Army 36
Newton, Isaac 48

Parliament 28, 30, 31, 34, 35, 36, 37, 38,
    40, 41, 53, 56, 57
Parr, Catherine 13
Pepys, Samuel 45, 47, 57
plague 44–5, 57
Pope, the 12, 16
Protestant church 16, 21 *see also* religion
Puritans 38, 40, 42

Reformation, the 16–7
religion 12, 16–7, 18, 19, 21, 23, 26, 30,
    34, 38, 40–1, 57
Restoration, the 38
Roman Catholic Church 12, 16, 19
    see also religion
Roundheads 34–7, 57
Royalists *see* Cavaliers

science 38, 48, 56
Seymour, Jane 12
Shakespeare, William 32–3
ships 14–5, 24–5, 26–7, 43, 56
Spanish Armada 26–7, 57

taxes 34
theatre 32–3, 38–9, 40
trade 14, 42–3, 50

war 14–5, 26–7, 36, 56
Wars of the Roses 8, 57
William III *see* Mary II, Queen and
    William III
Wren, Sir Christopher 47